This Book Belongs to _____

Let's get some things straight before I get old and uncool.

RULES *for* MY UNBORN SON

WALKER LAMOND

St. Martin's Griffin ⚋ *New York*

www.stmartins.com

Book design by Charles Kreloff

Library of Congress Cataloging-in-Publication Data

Lamond, Walker.
    Rules for my unborn son / Walker Lamond—1st ed.
        p. cm.
ISBN 978-0-312-60895-8
1. Men—Conduct of life—Miscellanea. 2. Fathers and sons—Miscellanea. I. Title.
    BJ1601.L36 2009
    395.1'42—dc22

                                                              2009028682

First Edition: November 2009

10 9 8 7 6 5 4 3 2 1

PHOTO CREDITS

Page 3: MGM/Photofest; **Page 9:** Cinema 5/Photofest; **Page 15:** Fox Photos/Getty Images; **Page 21:** Mary Evans Picture Library; **Page 29:** Claridge Pictures/Photofest; **Page 38:** B. Taylor/ ClassicStock.com; **Page 45:** United Artists/Photofest; **Page 55:** Bettmann/Corbis; **Page 62:** Liaison/Getty Images; **Page 66:** Photofest; **Page 69:** Bettmann/Corbis; **Page 72:** Alan Grant/ Getty Images; **Page 76:** E. Anheuser/WHS/ClassicStock.com; **Page 80:** Didoer Crozen; **Page 83:** American Stock/Getty Images; **Page 86:** © H. Armstrong Roberts/Corbis; **Page 90:** Photo by Express/Getty Images; **Page 95:** Bert Hardy/Getty Images; **Page 101:** American Stock Photo/ClassicStock.com; **Page 107:** Redferns/Getty Images; **Page 110:** Lambert/ Getty Images; **Page 113:** H. A. Roberts/ClassicStock.com; **Page 121:** Jan Tonnesen; **Page 125:** Photofest; **Page 128:** Rosemary Matthews/Getty Images; **Page 138:** © Bettmann/Corbis; **Page 145:** © Jack Moebes/Corbis; **Page 148:** Hulton Archive/Getty Images; **Page 151:** www .cksinfo.com; **Page 165:** Bettmann/Corbis; **Page 171:** The PSA History Museum—www.JwtPSA .com; **Page 181:** Fred G. Korth/Getty Images; **Page 185:** Time Life Pictures/Getty Images; **Page 190:** Charles Fenno Jacobs/Getty Images; **Page 195:** Hulton Archive/Getty Images

for ARTHUR

INTRODUCTION

*B*oys need rules. *No Spitting. No Swimming. No Fighting.* We don't always like them, but for the most part, they are necessary. Rules keep us safe, eliminate uncertainty, and encourage harmonious social interaction. *Yield to Pedestrians. Black Tie Required.* They are the simplest and most effective way to pass down tried and true institutional knowledge from one generation to the next. In short, rules are GOOD!

But somewhere along the way, rules got a bad name. People wanted freedom. Authority was questioned, rules were broken, dress codes banished! Rules were seen as antiquated obstacles to individualism and progress. Barbers were ignored, ties packed away. And the game of life suddenly got a bit sloppier, more uncertain, and even a bit less fun.

My father rarely wore socks, a sartorial quirk made permissible by the fact he was often the best-dressed gentleman in the room. This perhaps best exemplifies his approach to life. A vigorous dancer, a dedicated sportsman, and the tireless life of any party, he understood that a man of strong character, who took pride in his appearance and behavior, was given the most liberty to have fun. And so he had rules. Many of them came from his father, and presumably his father before that. They governed everything from his dress to his business dealings to a day at the ballpark and were based on the notion that there are certain things a Good Man does and certain things he does not do. My father was a Good Man. And he was the kind of father I aspired to be. He passed away shortly after my twenty-second birthday.

This small book began simply as a way to preserve the lessons my father had taught me and perhaps, add my spin on what makes a Good Man. I hoped to have a son of my own one day, so I thought it best to write it all down before the mayhem of actual fatherhood made me too soft or too sanctimonious, and most importantly, before my own childhood was too distant in the rearview mirror. It would be a father-to-be's promise to his unborn son: "To get some things straight before I get old and uncool."

Of course, the list needed a bit of updating. My dad could fold a mean pocket square, but he didn't have much to offer on Internet etiquette. As the list grew, however, what struck me was how many of my father's rules stood up unchanged—even for a recovering hipster living in New York. *Rules for My Unborn Son* became a set of instructions for being a good man and a good father, not just a list of commandments for any future progeny.

My father and I are not the first men to attempt to define and defend the qualities that make up the modern gentleman. In the book I acknowledge the influences of some very fine men who have offered wise and practical advice through the ages either through their words (Benjamin Franklin, Buckminster Fuller, Mark Twain) or their example (Fred Astaire, Jack Kennedy, David Bowie). Some of the advice the reader may have heard before. And I should hope so, as many of the rules are distillations of some universal lessons in ethics and etiquette. I have made efforts to cull the classics from the outmoded. After all, all that is old is good. However, what I hope makes *Rules for My Unborn Son* unique is the inclusion of lessons drawn from my own experiences—the good, the bad, and the ugly. The rules included herein may evoke from the reader a hearty endorsement or a spirited objection. Or perhaps inspire a sentimental journey back into the reader's own childhood. And maybe, for a particular kind of discerning young parent, *Rules for My Unborn Son* will be just what it says it is—a good old-fashioned book of rules for you and your family. I hope it proves useful.

—Walker Lamond
Washington, D.C.

When in doubt, wear a tie.

———∞∞∞———

Ride in the front car
of a roller coaster.

———∞∞∞———

See movies on the big screen.

———⁓———

Men with facial hair have
something to hide.

———⁓———

Be a vigorous dancer.

*However, you're under no obligation
to join a conga line.*

Be a strong swimmer,
especially in the ocean.

———✺———

Avoid gossip.

———✺———

Don't waste time with
a fancy watch.

———◦∕◦∕◦———

Talent is learned.
Learn to sing.

———◦∕◦∕◦———

Stand up for the little guy.
He'll remember you.

———◦∕◦∕◦———

Be careful what you set your heart upon,
for it will surely be yours.

—James A. Baldwin

Avoid affectations, lest
they become habits.

———∽∽∽———

Buy seasonal fruit from
your local stand or bodega.

———∽∽∽———

Don't attempt a dialect other than your own,

unless it's in the script.

Men should not wear sandals.

Ever.

On stage is no time to be shy.

Speak up.

Start a band.

A T-shirt is neither
a philosophy nor an
advertisement. It's a shirt.
Wear it plain.

Know her dress size.
Don't ask.

On occasion, pick up the tab.

Don't poke fun at
contemporary art.
Put it in context.

Don't spit on the sidewalk.

———◦/◦/◦——

The key to good
photography is not
timing. It's editing.

———◦/◦/◦——

Don't be shy in the locker room.
They are all thinking the same thing.

Be a good listener.
Don't just wait your turn to talk.

A vandal is the lowest form of scoundrel.

Yes Ma'am. No Sir.
No exceptions.

Spend time with your mother.

⟞⟞◦e◦⟝⟝

She's cooler than you think.

Choose your corner, pick away at it carefully, intensely, and to the best of your ability, and that way you might change the world.

—CHARLES EAMES

Know your furniture.
But never buy it all at once.

On a road trip, offer to buy
the first tank of gas.

Short pants are for little boys. Decide
for yourself when you are a man.

Always meet your date at the door.

———⚬⚬⚬———

Make a rock and roll pilgrimage.

———⚬⚬⚬———

Make a hipster's day.
Donate old clothes
to charity.

Close the door,
turn it up,
dork out.

Audition for a play.
Read for the lead.

———∞∞∞———

Never pack more than
you can carry yourself.

———∞∞∞———

Live in
New York.

———∞∞∞———

Offer to carry a woman's bags.

Especially your mother's.

Take the stairs.

—⦿⦿⦿—

Root for the home team,
even when they stink.

—⦿⦿⦿—

Have a reliable hangout.

Nothing good ever happens after 3 A.M.
I promise.

Sit in the front of the classroom.

Finish what you start,
especially books.

———◦◦◦———

There is rarely a time to raise your voice.
At the ball game is one.

———◦◦◦———

Never eat the same
meal twice in a row.

———◦◦◦———

Don't show off.
Impress.

Make sure your clothes fit properly.

A human being should be able to change a diaper, plan an invasion, butcher a hog, conn a ship, design a building, write a sonnet, balance accounts, build a wall, set a bone, comfort the dying, take orders, give orders, cooperate, act alone, solve equations, analyze a new problem, pitch manure, program a computer, cook a tasty meal, fight efficiently, die gallantly. Specialization is for insects.

—ROBERT ANSON HEINLEIN

At funerals, a dark suit is fine.
You shouldn't own a black one.

Don't loiter where there
is a dispute that does not
concern you.

Don't be a mooch.

———◦◦◦———

When speaking with a journalist,
choose your words carefully.

———◦◦◦———

Think about your answers,
then call them back.

Push-ups and sit-ups
are all you'll ever need to
build muscle.

———◦⁄◦⁄◦———

Never criticize a
book, play, or film
unless you have read or
seen it yourself. Art is
full of surprises.

———◦⁄◦⁄◦———

Support friends in the arts.
Especially if they stink.

—◦◦◦—

Learn to sail.

—◦◦◦—

The most expensive
restaurant is never
the best.

—◦◦◦—

Remember, the girl you're with is somebody's sister. And he's perfectly capable of kicking your ass.

Be a good passer, but don't forget to shoot.

Every time I see an adult on a
bicycle, I no longer despair for the
future of the human race.

—H. G. WELLS

Wear a sport coat
when traveling by plane.
It has easily accessible
pockets.

Spend as much time as you can on the water.

In a pinch, even a creek will do.

Keep your word.

Never side against your brother in a fight.

Memorize the Bill of Rights
and your favorite poem.

Respect fire.

Philanthropy is not measured in dollars and cents.

Never go out of your way to be on TV.

On a city sidewalk, walk
briskly and don't impede
pedestrian traffic.

Never hog a microphone.

Don't spend too much money on a haircut.

~~~

They don't last.

Take the train.

Run for student government at least once.

Let the axe do the work.

Feel free to crash a
tailgate party.

Lorem ipsum

You don't get to choose
your own nickname.

Lorem ipsum

Enough already.
Learn the rules of cricket.

———⦅∞⦆———

If you're going to reinvent yourself,

be original.

———⦅∞⦆———

Bodysurf.

———ගග———

Be subtle.
She sees you.

———ගග———

Give credit.
Take the blame.

———ගග———

Don't underestimate your fertility.

Write down your dreams.

When things go wrong—don't go with them.

—ELVIS PRESLEY

Keep your guard up.

Unless you have served
in the armed forces,
no fatigues.

The best thing you can give your
neighbors is a well-kept lawn.

Keep a schedule.

Experience the serenity
of traveling alone.

The one true measure of
a successful adventure is
returning home safely.

———⚬⚬⚬———

Call your mom.

———⚬⚬⚬———

Your best chance of being a rock
star is learning the bass.

———⚬⚬⚬———

When excusing yourself from the table, you need not give a reason.

———《ⁱ/ⁱ/ⁱ》———

If you have the right of way, take it.

———《ⁱ/ⁱ/ⁱ》———

If the maître d' mistakes you for someone famous, there's no rush to correct him.

———《ⁱ/ⁱ/ⁱ》———

Sympathy is a crutch.
Never fake a limp.

———◦✲◦———

Take your own pictures
at family events.

———◦✲◦———

Don't let the pictures
become the event.

When it comes to
opening presents, no one
likes a good guesser.

———◦◦◦———

Don't gloat. A
good friend will
do it for you.

———◦◦◦———

On matters of style, swim with the current.
On matters of principle, stand like a rock.

—THOMAS JEFFERSON

Don't tip the owner.
A handshake will do.

———◦/◦/◦———

Don't stare directly
into a dog's eyes.

———◦/◦/◦———

You can't cram for
a dental exam.

———◦/◦/◦———

Don't rush.

No coffee until you're sixteen.

———⟨∘/∘/∘⟩———

Never under any circumstances
ask a woman if she is pregnant.

———⟨∘/∘/∘⟩———

Make time for your mom on your birthday.

~~~

It's her special day, too.

Courage is not the lack of fear,

it is acting in spite of it.

—MARK TWAIN

Don't date the bartender.

Learn to pronounce French
words correctly.

Invest in great luggage.
The world will know that
you've arrived.

Be a regular at your
local flea market.

Let napping dads lie.

Don't be so eager to leave the kid's table.

If you choose to wear a tie, commit. Button your top button.

Offer your date the seat with the best view of the restaurant.

Never be the last one in the pool.

―――∽∽∽―――

Keep a garden.

―――∽∽∽―――

Surprise your dad at the office.

Trust me, whatever I'm doing is not as important as you.

The American, by nature, is optimistic. He is experimental, an inventor and a builder who builds best when called upon to build greatly.

—JOHN F. KENNEDY

Get back in touch with old friends.

Never turn down an invitation
to speak in public.

Eat more fish.

Do your own bicycle repairs.

Order dessert.

Don't shout out requests
at rock shows.

Have a signature look.

Be a good wingman.

—◦◦◦—

When selling tickets,
take face value.

—◦◦◦—

Don't stare.
People-watch.

—∽∘∽—

Protect your privacy,
especially when you're famous.

—∽∘∽—

Keep your eye on the ball and follow through.

In sports and in life.

Address anyone who carries a
firearm professionally
as sir or ma'am.

Explore the branches of your
family tree. You never know what
you might find.

Sleep with the window open.

———◦◦◦———

If you drop change, pick it up.
Even the pennies.

———◦◦◦———

Don't pose with booze.

———◦◦◦———

Make your own costume.

Hide not your talents. They for use were made. What's a sundial in the shade?

—BENJAMIN FRANKLIN

You aren't done raking until you've played in the leaf pile.

—⟨ᴏ⁄ᴏ⁄ᴏ⟩—

Never respond to a critic in writing.

—⟨ᴏ⁄ᴏ⁄ᴏ⟩—

Know the difference between arts and crafts.

—⟨ᴏ⁄ᴏ⁄ᴏ⟩—

Fish don't
have eyelids.
Cast into the
shade.

—◦◦◦—

Never swing at the first pitch.

No man bats a thousand.

Don't settle for a store bought cake.
Bake!

Surround yourself with smart people.

Don't be a snob.

*I not only use all the brains that I have,
but all that I can borrow.*

—WOODROW WILSON

When fishing, practice catch

and release.

If the teacher forgets to assign homework,

keep quiet.

Take her picture.

Don't ride your bike on the sidewalk.

—⟳⟳⟳—

Stand up to bullies.
You'll only have to do it once.

—⟳⟳⟳—

If you've made your point,
stop talking.

―――⊙⊘⊙――

Watch your language at the ballgame.

―――⊙⊘⊙――

Sit for a portrait.

―――⊙⊘⊙――

Always keep a recent photograph
of yourself on file in case of emergencies
or unexpected notoriety.

Get your pumpkins from
a pumpkin patch.

—∽∾∽—

Own a wool
flannel suit.

—∽∾∽—

Have a pen pal.

Admit when you are wrong.
Mean it.

If you spot a teacher outside of school,
leave him be.

Don't sabotage the family portrait.

Smile please.

Courtesy is as much a mark of a gentleman as courage.

—TEDDY ROOSEVELT

Don't personalize your license plates.

———∾∾∾———

If you offer to help, don't quit until the job is done.

———∾∾∾———

When it's time to sing in church, SING!
It's a great time to practice.

Wear freshly laundered pajamas.

If it looks like rain, carry an umbrella.
She'll thank you.

Cary Grant has no need for Gore-Tex.

The young man knows the rules, but the old man knows the exceptinos.

—Oliver Wendell Holmes, Sr.

Be precise.

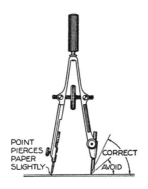

POINT
PIERCES
PAPER
SLIGHTLY

CORRECT

AVOID

Identify your most
commonly used word or phrase
and eliminate it.

Stay Busy. There is always
something that could use a
fresh coat of paint.

If you attend a late-night after-party,
have an exit strategy.

On Sunday morning,
a gentleman gets dressed.

Remember, it's the first day of the week,
not the last.

There is never an excuse
for stealing someone's cab.

—⟨∞⟩—

When you're older,
coach.

—⟨∞⟩—

Look people in the eye when you
thank them, especially waiters.

Choose a window seat
and enjoy the view.

Twice a year, write
down your goals.

No gang is complete
without one cool girl.

Hang artwork
at eye level.

There is no need to tell anyone you
are leaving the bar.

Always do sober what you said you'd do drunk. That will teach you to keep your mouth shut.

—ERNEST HEMINGWAY

Keep a well-stocked bar.

———

Read before bed every night.

———

Never post a picture online you wouldn't feel comfortable showing your mother, your boss, and the dean of admissions.

———

You will have a love life one day.

Be discreet.

Don't throw sand or, when
you're older, mud.

———∽∽∽———

Don't panic.

———∽∽∽———

When singing karaoke,
choose a song in your range.

———∽∽∽———

Thank the bus driver.

Go down fighting.

If you're playing a poker game and you look around the table and can't tell who the sucker is, it's you.

—PAUL NEWMAN

Keep your passport current.

Become an expert in something.

Write letters.
On paper.

Be careful what you put in writing. You can't take it back.

———◦∞◦———

There is exactly one place where it is acceptable to wear gym clothes.

———◦∞◦———

Mr. Bowie prefers trousers
to tracksuits.

Never ask about another
person's grades or salary.

———◦◦◦———

To execute a proper tackle, lower
your shoulder, not your head,
and remember to wrap up.

———◦◦◦———

Cite your sources,
even online.

⟡

Whistle.

⟡

Never push someone off a dock.
The view is better when you're not
afraid of who is behind you.

⟡

Offer to take a stranger's picture.

Work quickly.

Help a buddy move.

———∞∞∞———

Don't boast about projects in progress.
Celebrate their completion.

———∞∞∞———

Until you are a doctor, never
answer your phone at the table.

⸺◦◦◦⸺

If you make a mistake,
forgive yourself and move on.

⸺◦◦◦⸺

Be a good diver.

⸺◦◦◦⸺

Grace is an underappreciated
quality in men.

When you are a houseguest, be
sure to wake up before your hosts.

After lighting a firecracker,
stand back.

In a canoe, do your share of the work.

Go barefoot. It toughens the feet.

Make yourself useful on a boat. If you can't tie knots, fetch the beers.

Spend a summer waiting tables.

Always keep a good joke handy.

Take your sunglasses off indoors. This
includes elevators and planes.

Don't salt your food until
you've tasted it.

———◦◦◦———

Never turn
down a girl's
invitation to
dance.

———◦◦◦———

Be true to your school.

—BRIAN WILSON

Play hooky.

Never skip practice.

Avoid air-conditioning,
especially at the beach.

Order the local specialty.

Don't boo.
Even the ref is somebody's son.

Enter a talent show.

Be like a duck. Remain calm on the surface
and paddle like hell underneath.

—MICHAEL CAINE

Drive across the country.
Don't rush.

Limit your time in California.

Never ask to be taken
out of a ball game.

If you aren't a starter,
stay close to the coach
and be ready to play.

⸺◦◦◦⸺

There's nothing wrong with musical
theater. Everything in moderation.

⸺◦◦◦⸺

Chicks dig Gershwin.

Don't have a girlfriend in college.

A man's luggage doesn't roll.

Learn to drive a stick shift.

Jump in with your clothes on.

Smile at pretty girls.

A wise man knows his way around a kitchen.

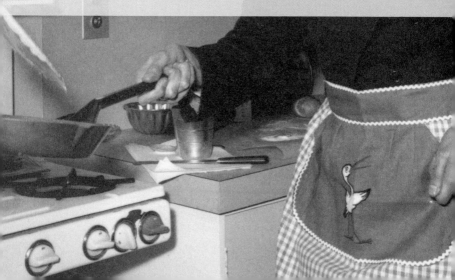

Have a signature dish,
even if it's your only one.

———⌇⌇⌇———

Be quick with a "Good morning."

———⌇⌇⌇———

Have a favorite song.
It doesn't have to be cool.

———⌇⌇⌇———

Be careful not to ogle girls at the beach. That's what sunglasses are for.

—⟨⟨⟨⟩⟩⟩—

If you ignore history, it will ignore you.

—⟨⟨⟨⟩⟩⟩—

If you get yourself arrested, call me.

You get one free pass.

There is more than one way to serve your country.

Drive a fuel-efficient car.

Don't be afraid to nominate yourself.

Be up to the task.

Make curfew.

Sneak out later to meet her.

A museum is a great place to beat a hangover.
It's cool, quiet, and full of water fountains.

Keep your room clean. One day you'll have roommates.

Do laundry often.
You won't need as many
clothes.

Never leave a job without
securing your next employment.

But when it's time to go,
don't hesitate.

Everything I've ever done was out of fear of being mediocre.

—CHET ATKINS

When it comes to shoveling snow, the earlier you start, the easier the job.

———— ✑∾∾✑ ————

Be nice to your sister. You are her cheerleader, confidante, and bodyguard.

———

Find yourself a
good hideout.

———

Always stop at a
lemonade stand. Tip well.

———

If you are tempted to wear a cowboy hat, resist.

We can't all be LBJ.

Know the proper
time to wear a tuxedo.
It's more often than you think.

The keys to throwing a
good party are a working
stereo, Christmas lights,
and plenty of ice.

Be cool to the younger kids.
Reputations are built over a lifetime.

Drive a vintage car before you are thirty.

Be able to wrench it yourself

Be confident on the subway.

On a night out with the boys,
never be the first to go home.

If you're going to quote someone,

get it right.

Know the proper time to chew gum.
It's less often than you think.

⎯◦/◦/◦⎯

On occasion, go to the
movies by yourself.

⎯◦/◦/◦⎯

Wait for your song to play
on the jukebox.

⎯◦/◦/◦⎯

Here's a rule I recommend.
Never practice two vices at once.

—TALLULAH BANKHEAD

Find your favorite painting.

Traveling to a foreign city is an
excuse to dress up, not down.

Dance with your partner, not at her.

But don't forget to lead.

The best thing to do in the rain
is be quiet and listen.

———◦◦◦———

Go all out on Halloween.

———◦◦◦———

Ask your mother
to dance.

———◦◦◦———

Take the time to get
a shoe-shine.

———⟨⟨⟨⟩⟩⟩———

Don't get fancy
about your beer
or coffee.

———⟨⟨⟨⟩⟩⟩———

Try a hairstyle you'll one day regret.

I'll get over it.

Don't let the ice-cream truck get away.

—∞∞∞—

Despite what your may hear,
not everyone's a winner. It doesn't
mean you shouldn't play.

—∞∞∞—

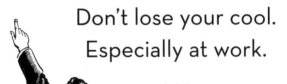

Don't lose your cool.
Especially at work.

———⌁◦/◦/◦⌁———

Some rules are made to be broken.
Jaywalking is not one of them.

———⌁◦/◦/◦⌁———

Participate in a good practical joke.

———⌁◦/◦/◦⌁———

When handling a frog, be gentle.

Offer your name when greeting
someone. Even good friends have
lousy memories.

—⟨∘∕∘∕∘⟩—

Be able to
identify all of
the trees on
your block.

—⟨∘∕∘∕∘⟩—

It is no use saying, "We are doing our best." You have got to succeed in doing what is necessary.

—WINSTON CHURCHILL

Never sit down on a ball field.
Take a knee.

Hustle.

If your mother is watching,
wear a helmet.

Keep hardback copies of your favorite books. Donate the rest to a local exchange.

Treat your body well. You'll be glad you did when you are a dad.

Be beholden to no one.
Pay in cash.

Remember
to thank
your hosts.

If you don't know what
a word means, ask.
Before it's too late.

———⚬⚬⚬———

Know your neighborhood
like the back of your
hand. Sometimes the best
adventures are in your own
backyard.

———⚬⚬⚬———

There is no better remedy
than a dip in the ocean.

——◦/◦/◦——

Trust the concierge.

——◦/◦/◦——

Marry the girl, you marry
the whole family.

<figure>⧯⧯⧯⧯</figure>

Never request a joke or impression.
They are never as good on command.

Suck it up.

If you have to make more
than one substitution,
order something else.

Wisdom begins with
an awe of nature.

Wit ought to be a glorious treat like caviar;
never spread it about like marmalade.

—NOËL COWARD

Attend lots of weddings.
Your friends will be there
and the food is always good.

Send postcards.

Read the good majority of a
newspaper every day.

—⦿⦿⦿—

Don't forget the
funny pages.

—⦿⦿⦿—

Collect things.

Draw what you see, not what
you think is there.

Exercise in the morning.
Bicycling to school or
work is a good idea.

—

Socks are not necessary in the summer,
no matter how formal the occasion.

Use the broiler.
It's an indoor grill.

Befriend your local
butcher.

———∞∞∞———

Sign the
guestbook.

———∞∞∞———

Own your own
baseball mitt and golf
clubs. All other athletic
equipment can be shared
or borrowed.

Offer your seat
to a woman, no matter
how old she is.

Get to know your
sister's boyfriends. I'll rely
on your opinion.

Never criticize the government of your

own country when you are abroad.

Be patient with airplane personnel.

It will pay off with better service.

Play organized football.

 You won't always be the
strongest or fastest. You
can be the toughest.

An hour with your grandparents is time well spent.

———⌘———

In the long run, loyalty trumps ambition every time.

———⌘———

Watch a lightning storm from a safe spot.
But watch 'em.

When caught in a riptide,
swim parallel to the beach.

Compliment your mom's cooking.

Wrap your own presents.
Aluminum foil works in a pinch and
you don't need tape.

Be a well-informed voter.

Don't forget your local elections.

Take it easy. But take it.

—WOODY GUTHRIE

Don't litter.
Ever.

⸺◦◦◦⸺

Honking your
horn won't make them
go faster.

⸺◦◦◦⸺

Drink rail liquor.

———ᴑᴑᴑ———

Minimize talking on the telephone.

———ᴑᴑᴑ———

Don't be afraid of
pickup games. It's the
best way to learn.

Keep iced tea in the fridge.
It's healthy, cold, and cheap.

If you can afford it, own
your own tuxedo.

If you absolutely have to fight,
punch first and punch hard.

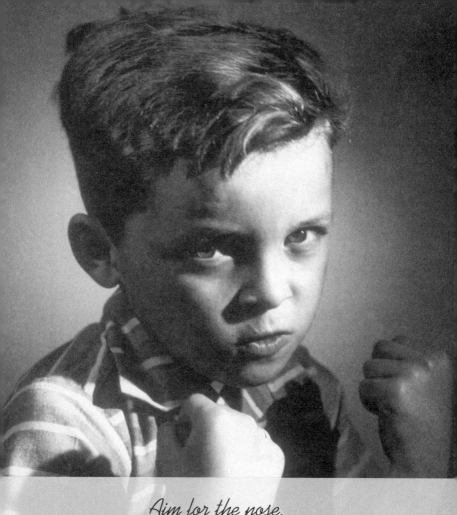

Aim for the nose.

No one likes a know-it-all.

Choose the correct screwdriver for the job.

When in the woods, be quiet.

Keep a copy of your letters. It will make it easier on your biographer.

Never let your correspondence fall behind.

—ABRAHAM LINCOLN

Eat more vegetables.
Takes care of the ticker.

—⟳⟳⟳—

Never talk during a
movie. Arrive early and go
for center seats.

—⟳⟳⟳—

Respect dress codes.
You'll have more liberty to be funny.

Learn to tie a bow tie.

Girls like boys who shower.

Write thank-you notes
promptly on personalized
correspondence cards.

In Monopoly, buy the
orange properties.

Don't renege on bets.
Better yet, don't gamble.

———⟨∞⟩———

When shaking hands,
grip firmly and look him in the eye.

———⟨∞⟩———

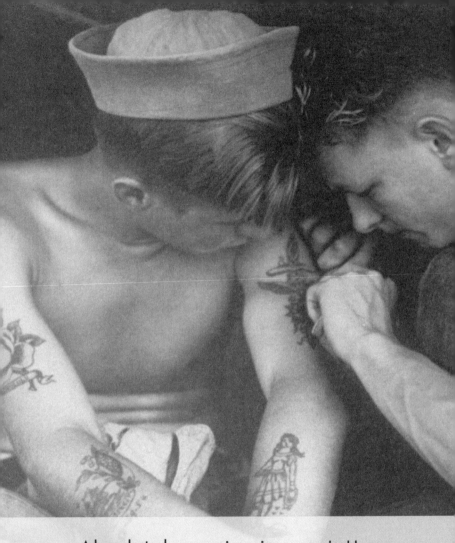

Absolutely no piercings or tattoos,
unless you are in the armed forces.

Spend time with your cousins.
You're more alike than you think.

Wear a pocket square.
The corner of a bed sheet
will work in a pinch.

If you get to thinking you are a person of some influence, try ordering somebody else's dog around.

—WILL ROGERS

You are what you do,
not what you say.

Don't flatten burgers on the grill.
It squeezes out all the juices.

It is not enough to be
proud of your ancestry.
Live up to it.

Don't make a scene.

Learn an instrument, preferably one that can be played at home in the company of friends.

Never switch a seating card.

When building a campfire,
choose deadwood from a tree,
not off the ground.

Keep a scrapbook. But avoid collage.

Jazz is for dancing.

Hold doors, pull out chairs,
easy on the swears.

—WILL SMITH

Bring your mitt to the ballpark.

Finish the
crossword.

Don't use a chisel for
anything other than its
intended purpose.

————◦/◦/◦————

When making an acceptance
speech, keep it short, lose the notes,
and thank your dad.

————◦/◦/◦————

Don't fight forces, use them.

—BUCKMINSTER FULLER

Don't be afraid of a little sun.

Follow instructions.
You'll be done in half the time.

————⌇⌇⌇————

Know when to ignore the camera.

————⌇⌇⌇————

For of those to whom much is given, much is required.

—Luke 12:48

Don't be afraid to ask out the
best-looking girl in the room.

Buy Regular Gas.

Nothing is
more important
than family.

You can never overdress.

APPENDIX

REQUIRED LISTENING
FOR BOYS

- ☐ Woody Guthrie . . . . "This Land Is Your Land"
- ☐ Nat King Cole . . . . "Straighten Up and Fly Right"
- ☐ Hank Williams . . . . "I'm So Lonesome I Could Cry"
- ☐ Little Richard . . . . "Long Tall Sally"
- ☐ The Beatles . . . . "Twist and Shout"
- ☐ Bob Dylan . . . . "It's All Over Now, Baby Blue"
- ☐ Four Tops . . . . "Reach Out (I'll Be There)"
- ☐ The Who . . . . "A Quick One"
- ☐ We Five . . . . "You Were On My Mind"
- ☐ The Monkees . . . . "Last Train to Clarksville"
- ☐ Otis Redding . . . . "These Arms of Mine"
- ☐ The Beach Boys . . . . "Good Vibrations"
- ☐ Elvis Presley . . . . "Suspicious Minds"
- ☐ Jimmy Cliff . . . . "Many Rivers to Cross"
- ☐ The Faces . . . . "Stay With Me"
- ☐ Jonathan Richman . . . . "Roadrunner"
- ☐ The Rolling Stones . . . . "Waiting on a Friend"

- [ ] Big Star . . . . "Thirteen"
- [ ] Tom Waits . . . . "Grapefruit Moon"
- [ ] Joni Mitchell . . . ."Free Man in Paris"
- [ ] New York Dolls. "Personality Crisis"
- [ ] Jackson Browne. . . . . "These Days"
- [ ] Gordon Lightfoot. . . . . "Sundown"
- [ ] David Bowie . . . ."Young Americans"
- [ ] Hall & Oates . . . ."Rich Girl"
- [ ] Billy Joel . . . ."Movin' Out"
- [ ] Cheap Trick. . . . . "Surrender"
- [ ] Elvis Costello . . . . "Peace, Love and Understanding"
- [ ] The Ramones . . . ."I Wanna Be Your Boyfriend"
- [ ] R.E.M.. . . . ."Radio Free Europe"
- [ ] Joe Jackson . . . . "Step Out"
- [ ] Big Country. . . . ."In a Big Country"
- [ ] Prince. . . . . "Let's Go Crazy"
- [ ] The Replacements. . . . . "Waitress in the Sky"
- [ ] The Pogues . . . ."Fairytale of New York"
- [ ] The Smiths . . . . "Girlfriend in a Coma"
- [ ] The Jayhawks. . . . ."Nevada, California"

ESSENTIAL READING FOR BOYS

- ❏ Rudyard Kipling . . . . *Just So Stories*
- ❏ L. Frank Baum . . . . *The Wonderful Wizard of Oz*
- ❏ Robert Westall . . . . *The Machine Gunners*
- ❏ Madeleine L'Engle . . . . *A Wrinkle in Time*
- ❏ Theodore Taylor. . . . . *The Cay*
- ❏ Jack London . . . . *Call of the Wild*
- ❏ William Golding . . . . *Lord of the Flies*
- ❏ S. E. Hinton. . . . . *The Outsiders*
- ❏ Mary Stewart. . . . . *The Crystal Cave*
- ❏ Robert Heinlein . . . . *Stranger in a Strange Land*
- ❏ Mark Twain . . . . *The Adventures of Tom Sawyer*
- ❏ Homer. . . . . *The Odyssey*
- ❏ Harper Lee . . . . *To Kill a Mockingbird*
- ❏ John Knowles . . . . *A Separate Peace*
- ❏ Erich Maria Remarque . . *All Quiet on the Western Front*
- ❏ Thor Hyerdahl. . . . . *Kon-Tiki*
- ❏ Claude Brown . . . . *Manchild in the Promised Land*

- ❑ Charles Darwin . . . . *The Origin of Species*
- ❑ Michael Shaara . . . . *The Killer Angels*
- ❑ F. Scott Fitzgerald . . . . *The Great Gatsby*
- ❑ Earnest Hemingway . . . . *The Sun Also Rises*
- ❑ Walker Percy . . . . *The Moviegoer*
- ❑ George Orwell *1984*
- ❑ Ken Kesey . . . . *One Flew Over the Cuckoo's Nest*
- ❑ Woody Guthrie . . . . *Bound for Glory*
- ❑ James A. Michener . . . . *Chesapeake*
- ❑ Patrick O'Brian . . . . *Master and Commander*
- ❑ Robert Penn Warren . . . . *All the King's Men*
- ❑ E. M. Forster . . . . *A Passage to India*
- ❑ Fyodor Dostoevsky . . . . *The Brothers Karamazov*
- ❑ John Cheever . . . . *Collected Stories*
- ❑ Richard Yates . . . . *Revolutionary Road*
- ❑ James Cain . . . . *The Postman Always Rings Twice*
- ❑ Sebastian Junger . . . . *The Perfect Storm*
- ❑ Michael Chabon . . . . *The Amazing Adventures of Kavalier and Clay*

NOTES

ACKNOWLEDGMENTS

I am grateful for the following people and institutions: Tumblr; Laura Wyss, a splendid photo researcher; my dedicated agent, Karen Gerwin; my talented editor, Alyse Diamond; and the entire staff at St. Martin's Press.

A number of people made significant contributions to the writing of this book, none as important as those by my wife, Colleen Lamond; my sister, Lizzy McMurtrie; and my mother, Betsy Lamond, the best teacher and friend a boy could hope for. Each is a testament to the truth that a father can teach you to be a man, but it is the women in your life that keep you alive and well. I am also grateful to my grandfather John C. Walker, a large number of friends whose character and talents inspire me daily, and the thousands of people who shared their own rules and advice for raising a good man.

I am especially grateful for the advice, example, and friendship of my father, Thomas B. Lamond, in whose memory I have dedicated this book.

ABOUT THE AUTHOR

Walker Lamond is a writer and television producer. His work has appeared on the Discovery Channel, National Geographic Channel, the Sundance Channel, and HBO. Lamond lives in Washington, D.C., with his wife and their son, who was born shortly after completion of this book.

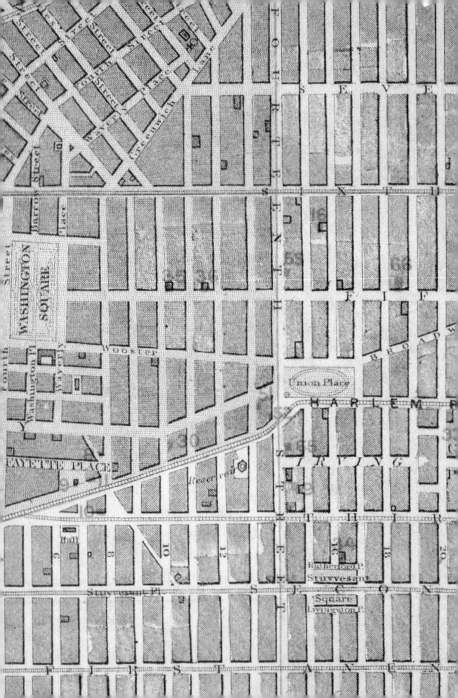

The Life and Times
~ of the ~
APPLE

Charles Micucci

ORCHARD BOOKS • NEW YORK

For little apple eaters, who ask lots of questions

Orchard Books
95 Madison Avenue, New York, NY 10016

Manufactured in the United States of America
Printed by General Offset Company, Inc.
Bound by Horowitz/Rae
Book design by Alice Lee Groton
10 9 8 7 6 5 4 3 2

The text of this book is set in 15.5 point Cheltenham Light.
The illustrations are watercolor and pencil reproduced in full color.

Library of Congress Cataloging-in-Publication Data
Micucci, Charles.
  The Life and times of the apple / by Charles Micucci.
    p. cm.
  Summary: Presents a variety of facts about apples,
including how they grow, crossbreeding and grafting techniques,
harvesting practices, and the uses, varieties,
and history of this popular fruit.
ISBN 0-531-05939-1. — ISBN 0-531-08539-2
1. Apple—Juvenile literature. [1. Apple.] I. Title.
SB363.M45 1992   634'.11—dc20   90-22779

Contents

The Life of an Apple

The apple is one of the most popular fruit trees in the world. Apple trees grow on every continent except Antarctica. In the United States alone, there are an estimated thirty million apple trees.

An apple tree may grow to be forty feet high and live for over a hundred years. But it always begins with one small seed.

Most apple cores have ten seeds. Usually, two seeds lie in each of the core's five chambers.

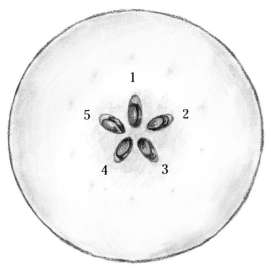

*horizontal cross section
of an apple*

Even though an apple seed is only ¼ inch long and weighs less than ¹⁄₁₀₀th of an ounce, it could grow to be as tall as a four story building.

Fruits that have seeds in a core are called pomes. Apples and pears are pomes.

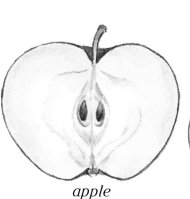

apple

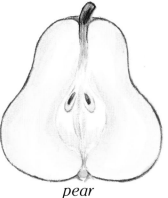

pear

Apples are a member of the rose family. So are pears, peaches, plums, and cherries.

Planting Apple Seeds

If you planted a seed from a big, red, juicy apple, a tree might grow, and it might bear fruit. But an apple from that tree would be different from your original apple. It probably wouldn't be as big, red, or juicy, and probably wouldn't taste as good. Why?

Apples reproduce through a process called cross-fertilization. The pollen from one apple blossom fertilizes another apple blossom. This fertilized flower then turns into an apple that will produce seeds with characteristics of both parent apples. Even though your apple is big, red, and juicy, its seeds might develop into trees bearing green or yellow apples of any size or shape.

Cross-fertilization of apples

If you plant the seed from a big, juicy apple and it grows into a tree, what kind of apple will it bear?

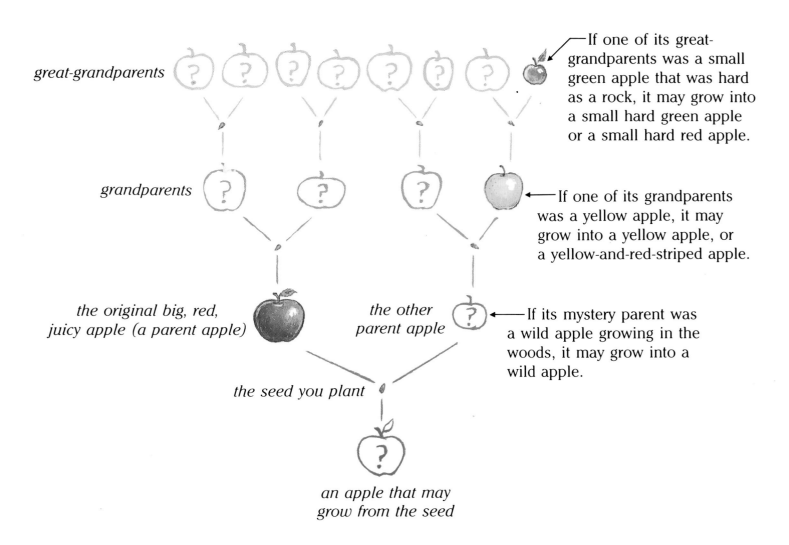

great-grandparents

If one of its great-grandparents was a small green apple that was hard as a rock, it may grow into a small hard green apple or a small hard red apple.

grandparents

If one of its grandparents was a yellow apple, it may grow into a yellow apple, or a yellow-and-red-striped apple.

the original big, red, juicy apple (a parent apple)

the other parent apple

If its mystery parent was a wild apple growing in the woods, it may grow into a wild apple.

the seed you plant

an apple that may grow from the seed

With so many question marks in an apple's family tree, you would never be able to predict what kind of apple would grow from the seed of a big, red, juicy apple.

Grafting

Most apple growers want to be able to predict what type of apple they are growing. Instead of growing trees from seeds, they use a procedure called grafting.

Grafting allows apple growers to control the type of apple they raise. The most common methods of grafting are the *cleft graft* and the *bud graft*.

The cleft graft is used by many commercial growers. On a tree that is cleft grafted, all the apples will be the same.

The bud graft is used mostly by gardeners, and to convert wild apple trees into domestic apple trees. On the branch that grows from a bud graft, all the apples will be the same. So a creative gardener could grow a tree with many kinds of apples by bud grafting different kinds of apple buds onto it.

A cleft graft joins a scion (a tree branch) to a rootstock (a tree trunk with roots).

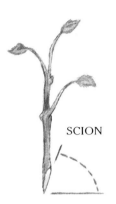

SCION

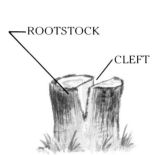

ROOTSTOCK

CLEFT

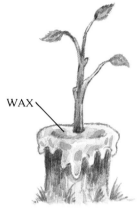

WAX

The end of the scion is cut at an angle.

A cleft is cut into the rootstock and wedged open.

The scion is inserted into the rootstock.

Wax is poured over the cleft to protect it from weather and insects.

A bud graft joins a bud (also known as a scion) to a rootstock or to another branch.

BUD (SCION)

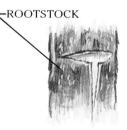

ROOTSTOCK

A bud is cut from a tree.

A T-shaped cut is made in the bark of a rootstock.

The bud is placed inside the T-shaped cut.

The bud and rootstock are wrapped with tape for support.

From these scions, a new apple tree will grow. In both types of grafting the scion determines what type of apples the tree will produce. For example, if the scion is from a Granny Smith apple tree, then all the apples will be Granny Smith apples.

Apple Blossom Time

Three to five years after grafting, an apple tree is ready to bear apples. In the summer tiny buds form on the branches. During the autumn, the buds develop and grow a covering of hair. The fuzzy hair protects the buds from ice and snow while the buds lie dormant during the winter months.

In the spring leaves sprout from the buds. Soon leaves fill the tree and little flower buds appear. Finally, as the days grow warm, the buds blossom into pink flowers.

apple buds in winter

apple buds in spring

It is important for apple buds to rest during the winter. That is why apple trees grow better in climates where winter temperatures drop below 45°F.

Apples can grow in colder climates than other fruit trees because they bloom later in the spring, minimizing damage to buds by frost.

FRUITS	BLOOM IN
CHERRIES	 MARCH—APRIL
PEACHES	APRIL
APPLES	MAY

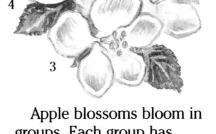

apple tree in bloom   *cherry tree in bloom*

Apple blossoms don't open until after leaves appear on the tree. On other fruit trees, such as the cherry tree, the flowers appear before the leaves.

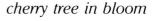

Most apple flowers are pink when they first blossom and gradually fade to white as they grow older.

Apple blossoms bloom in groups. Each group has five blossoms.

Parts of an Apple Flower

When you look at an apple flower, you see five pinkish white *petals* that extend from five green *sepals*.

If you cut an apple flower in half, you would see much more.

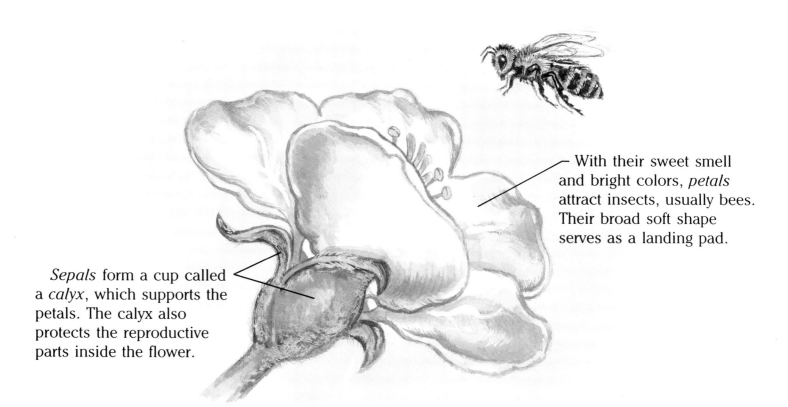

With their sweet smell and bright colors, *petals* attract insects, usually bees. Their broad soft shape serves as a landing pad.

Sepals form a cup called a *calyx*, which supports the petals. The calyx also protects the reproductive parts inside the flower.

The *pistil*, the female part of the flower, sits in the middle of the flower. The pistil includes the stigmas, styles, and the ovary.

Surrounding the pistil are many *stamens*. The male part of the flower, each stamen has a filament and an anther.

Five *stigmas*, special sticky surfaces where pollen collects, are at the top of the pistil.

Each *style* is attached to one stigma, holding it out of the flower so insects can brush against it.

Anthers produce an important yellow powder called pollen.

Nectar, a sweet liquid that attracts bees, is found in the center of the flower between the styles.

The *filament* is a tube that supports the anther.

An *ovary* rests at the base of the pistil. It is split into five sections.

Each section, called a *carpel*, contains two ovules.

Ovules are unfertilized apple seeds.

The *receptacle* is at the base of the flower where it meets the stem.

When *pollen* from the anthers of one apple blossom is transferred to the stigmas of another apple blossom, the ovules become fertilized and an apple begins to grow. This is called pollination. But apple flowers can't pollinate themselves. They need a helper—the honeybee.

Flight of the Honeybee

Honeybees, attracted by the smell and color of apple blossoms, fly from flower to flower searching for nectar, which they collect and make into honey, and pollen, which they make into bee bread.

Their only purpose is to feed themselves and their fellow bees. But in their travels some of the pollen they gather from one apple blossom accidentally brushes against the stigmas of another blossom. That's how bees help pollinate apple flowers.

When about one-fourth of the apple trees are blooming, a commercial apple grower hires a beekeeper who may bring in over a million bees to pollinate the orchard.

Honeybees do a special dance to let other bees know where they have found nectar and pollen.

Bee bread is a food mixed from honey and pollen that adult bees feed to three-day-old larvae, or baby bees.

How a bee pollinates an apple flower

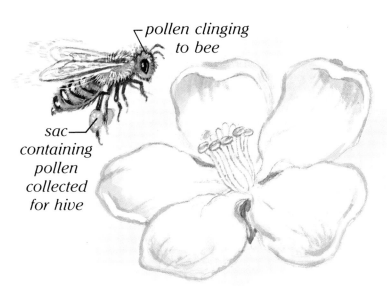

pollen clinging to bee

sac containing pollen collected for hive

A bee approaches a flower with pollen that it gathered from other flowers.

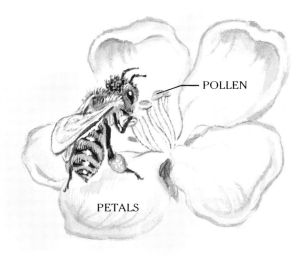

POLLEN

PETALS

The bee lands on the petals and searches for nectar and pollen.

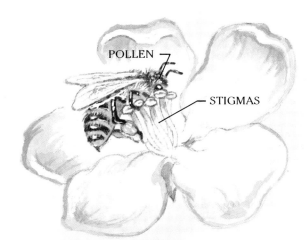

POLLEN

STIGMAS

As the bee gathers nectar, some of the pollen from other flowers accidentally brushes against this flower's stigmas.

pollen from other flowers

The bee flies away, leaving some of the other pollen behind.

From Flower to Apple

After the apple flower has been pollinated, the petals fall off, and the receptacle begins to bulge. Through the spring and summer, the little green bulge grows and changes shape until it begins to look like an apple. Toward the end of summer the apple changes color. Soon it will be ready for harvest.

Petals fall off.

The receptacle starts to swell.

The fruit becomes rounded and begins to look like an apple.

The apple reaches full size and starts to change color.

An apple has ten ovules. At least four of them have to be fertilized for an apple to grow, but unless all ten are fertilized, it will be lopsided.

In plants, leaves produce the energy required to grow fruit. Over fifty leaves are necessary to grow one apple.

All through the growing season, apples fall off the trees. But most of them fall about six weeks after bloom (June drop), and shortly before they're ripe (preharvest drop).

Sunlight causes apples to change color by causing a chemical reaction in the sugar of apples. These reactions produce red and yellow pigments in the apple's skin.

SUN

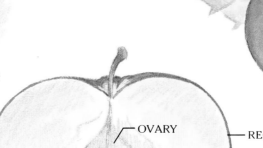

OVARY — RECEPTACLE

OVULES

SEPALS STAMENS

As an apple grows, the petals fall off, but the sepals, stamens, and pistil stay. You can still see the remnants of these parts in a ripe apple.

The sepals and stamens are at the bottom of an apple.

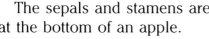

Inside an apple the pistil develops. The ovary grows into the core, and the ovules become seeds. When you eat an apple, you are actually eating the receptacle of the apple flower.

Harvesting Apples

In late summer and early autumn the apples are ripe and ready to pick. Today, in the age of spaceships, most apples are still picked just as they were in colonial times—by hand. Apple pickers, careful not to bruise the fruit, don't just yank apples off the tree. Instead, they gently cup each apple, then lift and twist it up and away from the tree. This insures that the apples will stay fresh longer and that new buds will grow on the tree next year.

The apple pickers place the apples in canvas bags they wear around their shoulders. From there, the apples are loaded into bins and shipped to market.

Apple pickers use a bag with a special bottom to hold the apples.

When the bag is full . . .

. . . they unsnap the bottom and empty the apples into a bin.

The largest quantity of apples is picked in October. That is why October is officially known as Apple Month.

Although most apples are picked by hand, some growers use mechanical pickers, which shake the fruit from the tree. Those apples are made into applesauce and juice.

Today some apple growers raise dwarf apple trees. Dwarf trees don't take up as much space as normal apple trees. A grower may be able to plant over 500 dwarf trees per acre, versus 27 per acre for some larger trees. And that means more apples at harvest.

full-size apple tree   *dwarf apple tree*

In addition to a test tasting, modern apple growers use many instruments that tell them when is the best time to pick apples.

A pressure gauge measures an apple's firmness.

A refractometer measures an apple's sugar content.

A computer calculates the climate, length of growing season, and other factors that may influence the apple's growth.

The Many Uses of the Apple

At market apples are cleaned and sorted according to type, size, and color. Ideally, only the best apples are sold fresh. Small apples, or those with imperfections such as bruises, are mashed into applesauce or pressed into apple juice. Because of their taste, nutritional qualities, and year-round availability, apples are used in more products than any other fruit.

pies

cakes

apple butter

turnovers

caramel apples

apple bread

applesauce

vinegar

in salads

juice and cider

The Pennsylvania Dutch
have carved apple core
dolls for hundreds of years.

About one in five apples is
pressed into juice and cider.

At Halloween witches and
goblins bob for apples.

Over half the apples grown are eaten fresh.

The Romans cooked apples in recipes.

Eating apples is healthy. They
contain vitamins A and C, and are
a good source of potassium. The
pectin in apples lowers cholesterol.
And eating apples regularly may
help reduce tooth cavities.

How Many Apples?

Each year there are over two hundred million bushels of apples grown in the United States and over a billion bushels grown worldwide. The leading apple-producing states are Washington, New York, and Michigan. The leading apple-producing countries are the Soviet Union, the United States, France, and Germany.

A billion bushels grown worldwide equals about 112 billion apples. That's 22 apples for every person in the world.

Apple production is measured in bushels. There are 112 medium six-ounce apples in a bushel. One bushel of apples weighs 42 pounds.

Most of the apples in the U.S. grow in those areas covered in apples on the map.

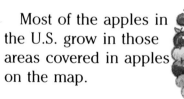

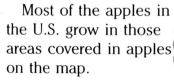

The U.S. exports over six million bushels of apples, more than all the apples grown in West Virginia.

Apples are the second most valuable tree fruit crop raised in the U.S. Oranges are the first.

Leading apple-growing states

Each basket equals one million bushels of apples.

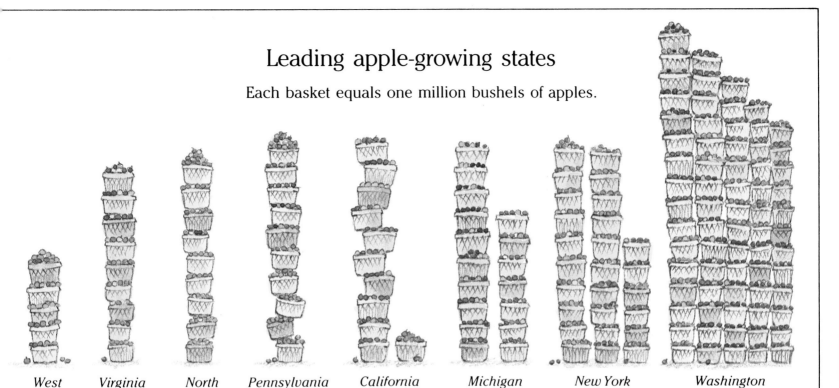

West Virginia | Virginia | North Carolina | Pennsylvania | California | Michigan | New York | Washington

Leading apple-growing countries

Each basket equals ten million bushels.

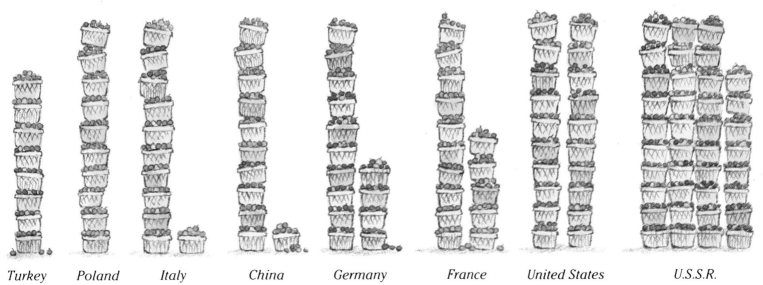

Turkey | Poland | Italy | China | Germany | France | United States | U.S.S.R.

Apple Varieties

Although there are almost 10,000 kinds of apples, only a few are raised commercially. In the United States alone, over half the apples grown are Delicious, Golden Delicious, and McIntosh.

Delicious apples total one-third of the apples raised in the U.S. Sweet and juicy, they're usually eaten fresh out of hand.

Golden Delicious apples are the most popular yellow apples in the U.S. They're good in pies or eaten fresh.

McIntosh apples are popular in the U.S. and Canada, eaten fresh or perhaps in applesauce. They serve as parent to some newer breeds such as the Cortland.

In colonial times, apples were called such fanciful names as Winter Banana, Melt-in-the-Mouth, and Westfield Seek-No-Further.

Winesap apples were grown by early pioneers for apple cider. Today they are raised in the Northwest and in the Appalachian Valley.

Gravenstein apples are thought to have originated at Castle Gravenstein, Germany (now part of Gråsten Slot, Denmark) in the 1600s. They're still grown in Europe and the U.S.

Granny Smith apples have a tart taste and are often baked into pies. They're usually grown in Australia, Chile, New Zealand, and South Africa.

Rome Beauty apples, because of their large size, may be cored, filled with raisins, and baked in the oven.

Cox's Orange Pippins are famous for their orange color. They are one of the most popular apples grown in England.

Cortland apples are used in salads because they don't turn brown as quickly as other apples do when they're sliced.

Newtown Pippins were the first apples exported from America. In 1768, some were sent to Ben Franklin while he was visiting London.

York Imperial apples have an odd, lopsided shape, as if they are leaning over.

Jonathan apples are eaten fresh, baked into pies, and processed commercially into a wide range of products.

Rhode Island Greening apples are excellent for baking in pies because they don't wilt and turn mushy when heated.

All the apples on this page are domestic apples. There are also about thirty kinds of wild apples in the world. They tend to be small and sour, but birds love them.

The Times of the Apple

Apples have been growing on earth for over two and a half million years. People of prehistoric times ate wild apples they picked from Asian forests. Later in the Stone Age, lake villagers in what is now called Switzerland started preserving apples, thus making it possible for people to eat apples all year long.

An apple time line

2,500,000 B.C.	100,000 B.C.	20,000 B.C.	400 B.C.	50 B.C.–

Apples are believed to have originated in Asia, near the Caspian Sea.

Stone Age lake dwellers preserved apples by drying them in the sun.

Rome conquered Europe and took the apple as far north as England.

Prehistoric people ate wild apples that tasted bitter and were only the size of a strawberry.

The Greeks grafted apples. They had 7 varieties of domestic apples.

While apples were once grown only from seeds, in the fourth century B.C. the Greeks started grafting apple trees. When ancient Rome expanded its empire, it spread the technique of grafting across Europe, including England. As England's gardens flourished, so did the apple. It was natural that, when colonists came to America, they brought apples and apple seedlings with them.

| A.D. 50 | A.D. 100 | Middle Ages | 1307 | 1600s |

Building on Greek techniques, Romans continued grafting apples. They had 36 domestic apple varieties.

Apples were grown throughout Europe.

Isaac Newton discovered the law of gravity while sitting beneath an apple tree.

Under threat by a tyrant, William Tell shot an apple off his son's head.

European ships sailed for America with apples on board.

27

In the 1800s Washington State apple growers east of the Cascade Mountains started irrigating their orchards. Today Washington is the leading apple-growing state.

In 1893 Iowa, a state known for its corn, became the birthplace of the U.S.'s most popular apple—the Delicious.

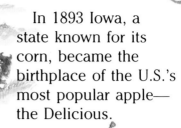

"Go West, Young Apple!"

The Europeans landed in North America, many with their own apples and apple seedlings. The Dutch shipped apple seedlings to New Amsterdam, which is now New York. The French started orchards in Canada. And the British colonists planted apples, from Newfoundland to Virginia. Then, as pioneers moved west, so did the apple.

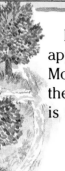

Some Indians planted apple trees around their villages.

Pioneers brought apples west in covered wagons.

During the late 1600s, Franciscan priests planted orchards in New Mexico, then part of the Spanish territories.

Cowboys fed apples to their horses as a special treat.

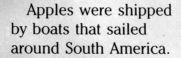

Apples were shipped by boats that sailed around South America.

Around 1800 John McIntosh discovered the first McIntosh apple trees in Ontario, Canada.

In 1629 the pilgrims of the Massachusetts Bay Colony received apple seedlings from England. The native crab apples were bitter, woody, chewy, and wormy.

Michigan named the Apple Blossom its State Flower in 1897.

Golden Delicious apples were born in the hills of West Virginia in 1914.

In 1730 the first apple nursery opened in Flushing, New York.

One of George Washington's hobbies was pruning his apple trees.

Thomas Jefferson experimented with several new apple varieties.

From 1795 to 1845 Johnny Appleseed planted apple seeds in Ohio, Indiana, Illinois, and Pennsylvania.

Virginia colonists grafted domestic apple branches onto wild apple tree trunks in 1647.

In 1901 Arkansas named the Apple Blossom its State Flower.

N
W   E
S

In colonial America apple cider was a popular drink before there was running water.

29

The Legend of Johnny Appleseed

Johnny Appleseed was born September 26, 1774, in Leominster, Massachusetts. His real name was John Chapman.

While in his early twenties Johnny moved to western Pennsylvania and soon started planting apple seeds. For fifty years he planted apple seeds in the Ohio Valley. He showed pioneers and Indians how to care for apple trees; they took his knowledge westward. Today many of the apple trees in Ohio, Indiana, Illinois, and Pennsylvania are descended from trees planted by Johnny Appleseed.

Johnny walked many miles barefoot to care for his apple trees, even in winter. He fashioned a tin pot into a hat, wore an old coffee sack shirt, and carried his seeds in a leather bag.

Johnny gathered his seeds from cider mills that were spread across the country.

Johnny didn't like to sleep indoors. He preferred to be outside, under the moon and stars. His seed bag was his pillow, and leaves and twigs were his blanket.

During the War of 1812, Johnny heroically raced through midnight forests to warn settlers that they were in danger.

A missionary of the Swedenborgian Christian religion, Johnny believed it was wrong to hurt another living being. He befriended wounded animals and was a vegetarian.

The apple has come a long way since prehistoric times. It has earned a place in world history. But the story of the apple doesn't stop here. Each spring billions of little apple buds across the globe add new chapters to the life and times of the apple.

"An apple a day keeps the doctor away!" is an old saying based on the nutritional qualities of the apple.

The phrase "The Big Apple" was originally a slang term for Harlem, popularized by jazz musicians and poets of the 1920s. Later, during the swing era of the 1930s, it became a popular dance. Today "The Big Apple" is a nickname for New York City.

"As American as apple pie." Americans like to think of themselves as wholesome, honest, and good—qualities also found in homemade apple pie.